Ripley's Believe It or Not!

Developed and produced by Ripley Publishing Ltd

This edition published and distributed by:

Mason Crest
450 Parkway Drive, Suite D, Broomall, PA 19008
www.masoncrest.com

Printed and bound in the United States of America

First printing
9 8 7 6 5 4 3 2 1

Ripley's Believe It or Not!
Extraordinary Art
ISBN: 978-1-4222-2778-7 (hardback)
ISBN: 978-1-4222-9039-2 (e-book)
Ripley's Believe It or Not!—Complete 8 Title Series
ISBN: 978-1-4222-2979-8

Cataloging-in-Publication Data on file with the Library of Congress

PUBLISHER'S NOTE
While every effort has been made to verify the accuracy of the entries in this book, the
Publishers cannot be held responsible for any errors contained in the work. They would
be glad to receive any information from readers.

WARNING
Some of the stunts and activities in this book are undertaken by experts and should not
be attempted by anyone without adequate training and supervision.

Ripley's Believe It or Not!®

Strikingly True

EXTRAORDINARY ART

www.MasonCrest.com

EXTRAORDINARY ART

Feast your eyes on these creations!

Read about the artist who inflates

dead animals, the 10-in (25-cm) stiletto

shoes made from elephant dung, and the

painter who uses his own blood in his work.

Art group LA Pop Art used all the words from the first 11 chapters of Alice in Wonderland *to create this illustration...*

Ripley's Believe It or Not! extraordinary art

Body of Work

Ripley's Ask

How did you start painting on people? I had been a conventional professional artist for 20 years, but I never felt satisfied with what I was creating. I kept searching for a style or a technique that would not only fulfill and push me, but that would also contribute to the evolution of contemporary art. I was in my mid-thirties before I considered bodypainting as the solution to my creative dilemma. I had painted on several bodies before and the idea of taking bodypainting seriously as fine art made the difference. Only a handful of artists had approached bodypainting as fine art before me, and this allowed for plenty of room to contribute.

How long can a bodypainting take to complete? The amount of time that my work takes to produce can vary greatly. Some of my pieces incorporate custom-painted backdrops and these can easily take a full day of work or more to create and complete. Other, simpler images require only a few hours to achieve. My average bodypainting takes about eight hours to complete and about 40 minutes to photograph.

What do you like about body art as opposed to more conventional painting? In the past 30 years, I've painted on almost every surface known to man and I can unequivocally state that nothing even comes close to the beauty and complexity of working on the human body. We are the most interesting and sophisticated entity in our known universe. I've chosen to not just artistically represent the human figure, I've purposefully decided to create directly on and with the beauty and soulfulness of the human being.

A closer look at these images reveals that they are all created using the human body. By painting directly onto skin, artist Craig Tracy of New Orleans, Louisiana, manipulates the natural shape of his models against a meticulously designed background, creating mind-blowing illusions without the use of computer trickery.

Craig uses photographs to plan the image and then models often sit for hours at a time as he applies the paint, with each painting taking on average one day to complete.

BUTTERFLY
Named after the butterfly shape visible on the nose of the panther, *Butterfly* was completed in one mammoth 24-hour session, with only one hour of sleep for Craig and his model.

IMMACULATE ▲
Immaculate features a hand-painted and airbrushed background. Once the models are in position, Craig adds the final paint to their body.

RIPLEY RESEARCH

Victor uses leaves from the maple-like Chinar tree, as they are particularly durable. The process takes around a month, involving as many as 60 individual steps. First he boils the leaf in water to soften it and remove any bacteria. Then he removes the layers of the leaf with a knife and needle, taking care to keep the delicate veins in place. Next he carefully cuts and sculpts the surface to create his chosen image. Then he brushes and shaves the leaf to make it appear transparent, coats it in an anti-aging treatment, dries it again, and finally waxes it before framing.

A NEW LEAF

Victor Liu collects dried old leaves from the streets around his home in Hebei Province, China, and very painstakingly carves into them beautiful images of subjects such as Barack Obama, Marilyn Monroe, the *Mona Lisa*, and the Statue of Liberty.

new york bears Joshua Allen Harris placed inflatable polar bears made from discarded plastic bags above ventilation grates in the New York City subway so that the animals inflated and deflated with the passing of underground trains.

daily grind Instead of paint or ink, Bend, Oregon, artist Karen Eland creates replicas of famous artworks with coffee. Since her first espresso painting in 1998, she has completed more than 90 illustrations—many of which incorporate coffee drinking—including *Leonardo da Vinci's Mona Latte*, *Whistler's Mocha,* and *Rodin's The Drinker*.

traveling bible A unique 1,500-page traveling Bible, written in 66 languages—one language for each book of the Old and New Testament—has toured more than 150 countries. The huge 15-lb (7-kg) book, which measures 18 x 12 in (45 x 30 cm), set off on its world tour from the Philippines in October 2008.

baseball mementos Mitch Poole, clubhouse manager with the Los Angeles Dodgers baseball team, turns milestones into mementos by painting significant game balls with details of the achievement. It is traditional for a clubhouse manager to retrieve the ball when an important hit, run, steal, or win takes place, and for more than 20 years Mitch has decorated hundreds of balls. Using acrylic paint, he writes the player's name, opponent, accomplishment, date, box score, and other information on the ball.

original nintendo In February 2010, a video-game collector paid $13,105 for an original Nintendo entertainment system and five game cartridges.

stage epic German producer Franz Abraham has created a stage version of the Roman epic *Ben-Hur* featuring 400 actors, 900 costumes, 50 scene designs, 46 horses, 120 doves, five chariots, two eagles, and two vultures. The action takes place in a 26,000-sq-ft (2,415-sq-m) arena covered with 10 in (25 cm) of sand. The production uses 30 mi (48 km) of cable, 250 moving lights, and 25 tons of sound equipment.

big business In Minneapolis, Minnesota, in 2009, entrepreneur Lief Larson presented a work contact with a giant business card that measured 60 x 34 in (150 x 85 cm).

CROCHET LIONS

English "crochetdermist" Shauna Richardson spent two years hand-crocheting three huge lions, each measuring 25 ft (7.5 m) long and 10 ft (3 m) high. She crocheted the skins in wool, accurately tracing the animals' muscular contours, over a polystyrene and steel framework. Shauna also crochets life-size pieces, which have included wild boars, bears, and baboons.

tattooed pigs Belgian artist Wim Delvoye tattooed pigs with Louis Vuitton designer logos for an exhibit called *Art Farm*. He tattooed the LV logos on the animals when they were piglets and watched the designs increase in size as the pigs' bodies grew.

some yarn! Over the period of a week, Austin, Texas, artist Magda Sayeg covered a Mexico City bus from front to back with brightly colored knitted yarn. She has also knitted woolen coverings for trees, car antennas, and signs in the United States, as well as for the Louvre Museum in Paris.

typed portraits Keira Rathbone of Dorset, England, uses manual typewriters—some up to 70 years old—as her paintbrushes to create portraits of famous people, including Barack Obama, Marilyn Monroe, and supermodel Kate Moss. After deciding which of her collection of 30 typewriters she wants to use, she turns the roller and selects different characters—numbers, letters, and punctuation—to make the required shapes.

tan art James Titterton of London, England, endured a full body wax and eight sunbed sessions to have a fish, a cockerel, and a ship's anchor bronzed onto his flesh. He masked off parts of his chest, arms, and legs with vinyl stickers of the various images before having the outlines tanned on to his skin. Dressed in only underpants, he then exhibited his tanned artwork at a gallery in Sussex.

naked hug More than 5,000 people took off their clothes and embraced each other in the nude on the steps of Sydney Opera House, Australia, in March 2010 for a photo shoot by American artist Spencer Tunick.

$11 million book A copy of the book *Birds of America*, written and illustrated by Haitian-born John James Audubon in the early 19th century, was sold for more than $11 million in December 2010. Only 119 complete copies of the large-format book, which has foldout pages measuring 39½ x 29½ in (100 x 75 cm), are in existence, and all but 11 of those are in museums and libraries. To obtain such accurate likenesses of birds, Audubon stalked his subjects across the United States and shot them before hanging them from wires and painting them.

behind the smile Dr. Vito Franco of the University of Palermo, Sicily, Italy, believes the enigmatic smile on the face of Leonardo da Vinci's *Mona Lisa* was the result of very high levels of cholesterol. After studying the painting closely, the doctor says he can detect a build up of fatty acids around her left eye.

sound your horn! A giant, working vuvuzela horn 115 ft (35 m) long and 18 ft (5.5 m) in diameter was installed above a highway in Cape Town, South Africa, in 2010.

Living Dolls

When British artist Boo Ritson tells her subjects she wants to paint them, she means it literally. Boo covers her human volunteers in layers of water-based paint to create giant action figures, which she then photographs. She specializes in American symbols, which means that as well as painting subjects such as cheerleader and cowboy living dolls, she has also applied the technique to donuts.

extraordinary art

Ripley's
Believe It or Not!®

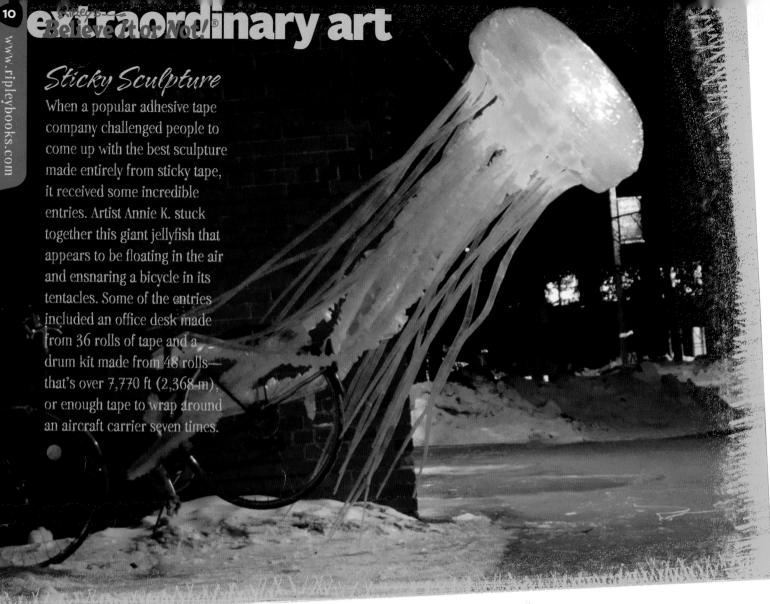

Sticky Sculpture

When a popular adhesive tape company challenged people to come up with the best sculpture made entirely from sticky tape, it received some incredible entries. Artist Annie K. stuck together this giant jellyfish that appears to be floating in the air and ensnaring a bicycle in its tentacles. Some of the entries included an office desk made from 36 rolls of tape and a drum kit made from 48 rolls—that's over 7,770 ft (2,368 m), or enough tape to wrap around an aircraft carrier seven times.

® **cardboard scream** Artist Mark Langan from Cleveland, Ohio, re-created Edvard Munch's haunting painting *The Scream* using discarded cardboard boxes. He spent 90 hours cutting up five old boxes with a craft knife and layering them to create a three-dimensional picture that measured 2.2 in (5.5 cm) deep. His cardboard creation sold for $2,500.

® **noncontact instrument** The theremin is an electronic musical instrument that is played without any contact from the player! Named after Russian professor Léon Theremin, who invented it in 1919, it consists of two metal antennae that sense the position of the player's hands and send corresponding electric signals to a loudspeaker.

® **microbial art** Dr. T. Ryan Gregory of the University of Guelph, Canada, is a pioneer of microbial art, where scientists design patterns by brushing fungi, deadly bacteria, and dye around a petri dish. He creates images by using a small paintbrush and E. coli in liquid medium. These are then allowed to grow in a laboratory incubator, but the "living paint" soon dies, so the pictures are only temporary.

DEAD FLIES

Magnus Muhr collects dead flies from windows and lamps around his house in Sweden, places them on white paper, draws in legs and a crazy background, and then photographs them. The photos show the insects appearing to dance, sunbathe, dive, ride horses, and perform acrobatic circus routines.

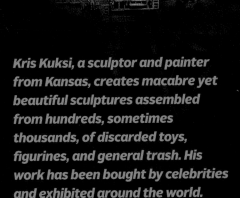

giant chair Furniture craftsman Radoslav Russev carved a wooden chair that was almost 15 ft (4.5 m) high and weighed more than 770 lb (350 kg). He made the oversized chair, which was placed in the main square of Razgrad, Bulgaria, from 70 cubic ft (2 cubic m) of pinewood.

leather portraits Welsh artist Mark Evans creates huge portraits of famous people—in leather. Using knives as his "brushes," he has scraped impressions of Muhammad Ali, Sir Winston Churchill, and model Naomi Campbell into leather hides. He discovered his talent by accident after spilling blood on a new leather jacket. He tried to repair it with a palette knife but scratched too hard and ended up etching a portrait of Jimi Hendrix onto the back of the jacket.

cereal-ism With the help of 150 students, high-school teacher Doyle Geddes of Smithfield, Utah, used 2 tons of breakfast cereal to create a massive reproduction of Vincent van Gogh's painting *Starry Night* measuring 72 x 90 ft (22 x 27 m).

board game In 2009, board-game fanatic Luanga Nuwame created a 900-sq-ft (84-sq-m) wooden board game based on the city of Mississauga, Ontario, Canada...with real people as the pieces. He also built a huge dice with which to play it.

washington's fine New York Society Library says George Washington owes it $300,000 in library fines. Its ledgers show that the first U.S. President borrowed two books that were due to be returned on November 2, 1789, but are now more than 220 years overdue.

costly comic A copy of the 1938 edition of *Action Comics No. 1* sold in March 2010 for $1.5 million on an auction website. The issue, which features Superman's debut, originally sold for 10 cents.

french anthem Claude-Joseph Rouget de Lisle composed "The Marseillaise" in 1792 in return for a bottle of wine. The tune became the anthem of French Revolutionaries and was later adopted as the French national anthem. Ironically, Rouget de Lisle was a royalist who was thrown into prison during the Revolution and narrowly escaped being guillotined.

observation test To help improve their powers of deductive observation, a group of New York City police officers visited the Metropolitan Museum of Art to discuss with an expert what conclusions they could draw from the contents of pictures by the likes of Caravaggio and Guercino.

many parts Bollywood actress Priyanka Chopra played all 12 characters in the 2009 movie *What's Your Rashee?* Each character was one of the 12 zodiac signs.

serenading sharks Andy Brandy Casagrande IV, an American wildlife cinematographer, strummed a waterproof guitar and played a song underwater to sharks off the coast of Mexico—without a cage. He penned "The Great White Shark Song" to raise awareness of shark conservation and decided the best way to make his point was to don scuba gear and play his tune in shark-infested waters.

Kris Kuksi, a sculptor and painter from Kansas, creates macabre yet beautiful sculptures assembled from hundreds, sometimes thousands, of discarded toys, figurines, and general trash. His work has been bought by celebrities and exhibited around the world.

Kris explains how Lies and Persuasion came together:

"My pieces are a collection of many different things. I started out by gathering miscellaneous figurines, small rocks, jewelry—anything I could incorporate. After I found some essential "supplies" that I felt were important for the individuality of the piece, I built a foundation, and everything after that is just assemblage. When it's all finished, the piece gets various coats of paint.

"Lies and Persuasion has so many little things in it and, interesting enough, the skull forms in the piece are actually the same skull split in half. I'll buy anything, anywhere, if I feel it's needed for a piece. I'd say that the whole assemblage, that is, the creation itself—withholding the mental preparation and shopping—lasted about a month."

TURN THE PAGE...

extraordinary art

ILLUSION CONFUSION

There is a lot more to this portrait of legendary artist Salvador Dali than meets the eye. It is in fact a large three-dimensional illusion, consisting of a shark, a bull's head, and a seal, among many other objects. These bizarre items appear to be randomly piled up but are actually meticulously placed to complete the image from just one perspective. Bernard Pras, the artist from Belgium, has been re-creating famous pictures out of junk for more than 30 years.

microscopic models Origami artist Mui-Ling Teh of Thornhill, Ontario, Canada, makes paper models so tiny—as small as 0.08 in (2 mm) long—that they look like a speck to the naked eye. She makes her microscopic models of objects such as birds, flowers, and airplanes with scissors and tweezers. She first began to experiment with origami at age ten when she made small models out of candy wrappers.

auto robot A 33-ft-tall (10-m) version of Transformer Optimus Prime made from the bodies and tires of old cars and motorcycles was unveiled at Beijing's Green Dream Park in 2010. The Autobot sculpture weighed six tons and was assembled from five truckloads of recycled parts.

huge hammock Hansy Better Barraza, a professor at Rhode Island School of Design, created a 33-ft-long (10-m) hammock, covering an area of 264 sq ft (24.5 sq m) in Boston, Massachusetts, in 2010. The sculpture consisted of 4,278 ft (1,304 m)—that's nearly a mile—of "rope" made from recycled bottles woven over curved steel pipes.

avid reader Nonagenarian Louise Brown from Dumfries and Galloway, Scotland, has borrowed 25,000 library books in her lifetime. She has read up to a dozen books a week since 1946 without incurring a single fine for late returns.

smelly issue Issue No. 23 of the German magazine *mono.kultur* was infused with 12 smells suggested by Norwegian scientist, artist, and odor expert Sissel Tolaas. Using a technique called microencapsulation, the smells were printed into the pages of the magazine, with the reader rubbing the paper to release them.

human ashes Dutch artist Wieki Somers makes 3-D printed sculptures of common household appliances—including bathroom scales, a vacuum cleaner, and a toaster—out of human ashes.

gallery blunder Polish experimental artist Leon Tarasewicz sued a gallery for $30,000 after it ripped up one of his paintings and threw it in a trash can in the mistaken belief that it was a large bunch of scrap paper used for getting excess paint off brushes. The 25-ft-high (7.6-m) exhibit had been on display in the gallery in Katowice, but staff thought that it had been left behind by decorators.

beef bikini For the September 2010 cover shot of Japanese magazine *Vogue Hommes Japan*, U.S. singer Lady Gaga wore a bikini made of raw meat.

Tasty Shoes Israel's Kobi Levi has designed shoes in the shapes of bananas, cats, shopping baskets, dogs, rocking chairs—and one pair with a pink stiletto heel that makes it look as though the wearer has stepped in a piece of chewing gum.

GLASS HOLOGRAMS

Using special pencils, multiple layers of painted glass, and between 14 and 30 glass panes, artist Xia Xiao Wan from Beijing, China, is able to transform ordinary 2-D glass into stunning 3-D holographic images.

playing with food Brazilian artist and photographer Vanessa Dualib creates cartoon animals from misshapen food and then takes pictures of them against appropriate backdrops before they go rotten. Among her 70 characters are radish mice, blowfruit fish, a potato dinosaur, and Pepe the pepper.

mosaic mural More than 130 artists and 500 children worked for three years to create a ceramic mosaic mural in Hanoi, Vietnam, that measures nearly 2½ mi (4 km) long. The brainchild of artist Nguyen Thu Thuy, the mosaic depicts images of Vietnam's history, life, and culture.

whistle-stop tour German guitarist Vicente Patiz drove more than 600 mi (960 km) to give concerts in eight countries—Germany, Belgium, the Netherlands, France, Luxembourg, Switzerland, Lichtenstein, and Austria—in just 24 hours.

bamboo dance More than 10,700 people assembled on March 12, 2010, to perform the Cheraw dance together in Aizawl, Mizoram, India. They spread out over an area of about 1¾ mi (3 km) to dance an eight-minute routine with bamboo sticks.

bargain buy A decade after buying 65 photographic plates at a garage sale in California for just $45, Rick Norsigian found that they could be the work of celebrated U.S. nature photographer Ansel Adams and therefore be worth around $200 million.

quick on the draw Singaporean artist Peter Zhou, aka Peter Draw, drew nearly 1,000 people nonstop, without food, for 24 hours.

Poo Shoes

British artist INSA created a pair of 10-in-high (25-cm) stiletto shoes with platforms made from elephant dung. He sourced the waste from the same family of elephants that provided the material for a famous series of elephant-dung collage paintings by Turner Prize-winning British artist Chris Ofili in the 1990s.

extraordinary art

Roll the Dice Ari Krupnik, a software engineer from Silicon Valley, California, builds mosaics of famous people from hundreds of dice, achieving different shades of gray according to which face is up. He created a portrait of revolutionary leader Che Guevara from 400 dice and one of George Orwell, author of *Animal Farm*, from 1,925 dice. He has also made a 3-D image of actress Uma Thurman from hundreds of M&M's®.

pretty paddies Each year, the farmers of Inakadate Village, Aomori Prefecture, Japan, use different-colored varieties of rice to create works of art spanning entire rice paddies.

blind draft U.S. novelist Kent Haruf writes the first draft of each of his books blind! He takes off his glasses, pulls a stocking cap down over his eyes, and types his words in darkness.

rubik's replica Five artists in Toronto, Canada, spent two months making a replica of Leonardo da Vinci's *The Last Supper* measuring 8½ x 17 ft (2.6 x 5.2 m), using 4,050 Rubik's cubes.

poetry booth Starting in October 2009, an old-style telephone booth in Yellow Springs, Ohio, served as a stage for poetry readings, light shows, and dance performances. People could walk into the booth, pick up the receiver, and listen to a recorded reading of short poems or simply create their own experimental artworks.

vast violin In 2010, a dozen workers in Markneukirchen, Germany, created a playable violin that measured 13 ft 11 in (4.3 m) tall, 4½ ft (1.4 m) wide, and weighed more than 220 lb (100 kg).

gum-wrapper dress Elizabeth Rasmuson of Garner, Iowa, made her 2010 high-school prom dress out of hundreds of gum wrappers that she and her boyfriend, Jordan Weaver, had been collecting for six months. She also made him a matching vest out of blue-and-white gum wrappers.

in the dark London's Tate Modern gallery unveiled its latest giant installation in 2009—40 ft (12 m) of pitch darkness. It was created by Polish artist Miroslaw Balka who said that the darkness was a metaphor for life.

party poopers U.S. rock band Kings of Leon had to abandon a concert at the Verizon Amphitheater, St. Louis, Missouri, in July 2010 after they were bombarded with pigeon droppings. An infestation of birds in the rafters above the stage led to bassist Jared Followill being hit several times during the band's first two songs, including in the face.

lego plane LEGO™ enthusiast Ryan McNaught built a $5,500 replica of the world's biggest passenger plane—the Airbus A380—with more than 35,000 bricks. It took him more than eight months to build the model, which is 7 ft (2.1 m) long and 6 ft (1.8 m) wide, in the garage of his home in Melbourne, Victoria, Australia.

garbage pictures Richard Broom of Lincolnshire, England, spent hours photographing litter along Britain's roadsides and posting them on an Internet blog in an attempt to get the government to tidy up the country—but his photos, including discarded paper cups, old cans, a broken toilet, and bottles of urine, proved so popular that they have turned into highly collectable art.

mini mansion Peter Riches of Hove, England, spent nearly 15 years creating an elaborately decorated doll house and sold it for $80,000—that's enough to buy a real home in some places. His miniature 23-room mansion boasted a music room with grand piano, a hand-crafted games room with snooker table, and a library with more than 1,000 individually bound books. He made the shell of the house from plaster and hand-etched 32,000 bricks on its walls. He cut the 5,000 roof tiles from cardboard. The finished house measured 4 ft (1.2 m) wide, 3 ft 3 in (1 m) high and 2 ft 7 in (80 cm) deep.

cloud graffiti U.S. pop artist Ron English created cloud graffiti in the skies above New York City in September 2009. He hired a skywriting plane and got it to spell the word "cloud" in puffy white dots several times over the city.

tiny tiger A Taiwanese artist has created a painted tiger sculpture that is smaller than a grain of rice. Chen Forng-Shean spent three months carving the 0.04-in-high (1-mm) tiger from resin. He has also made delicate miniature sculptures from sand, dental floss, rice, ant heads, and fly wings.

pinhead nativity In 2009, Italian craftsman Aldo Caliro sculpted a nativity scene—featuring hand-carved figures of the Virgin Mary, Joseph, and an angel, plus a tiny baby Jesus in his crib—on the head of a pin! He painted the figures with a single paintbrush hair. He had previously carved nativity scenes on a lentil and a coffee bean.

chalk drawing *Head of a Muse*, a simple black chalk drawing on paper by Renaissance painter Raphael, sold at an auction in London, England, for $47.9 million in December 2009.

long story It will be nearly 1,000 years before the cover of the May 2009 issue of *Opium* magazine can be read in its entirety. It will take that long for the successive layers of ink to degrade—at the rate of one word per century—thereby revealing a nine-word tale created by U.S. conceptual artist Jonathan Keats.

precise worker U.S. bestselling horror writer Stephen King, originally from Portland, Maine, writes exactly ten pages (around 2,000 words) a day, whether he's in a creative mood or not.

coffee cups At the 2010 Rocks Aroma Festival in Sydney, Australia, a team of artists created a 21 x 18 ft (6.5 x 5.5 m) coffee mosaic of Marilyn Monroe. They formed the image by filling 5,200 cups of coffee with 180 gal (680 l) of milk and 205 gal (780 l) of coffee to varying levels.

enormous shirt A team of South-African tailors worked nonstop for three weeks to make a T-shirt bigger than the Statue of Liberty. About 6.5 million stitches held together the 208 x 140 ft (64 x 43 m) shirt, using over 22,965 ft (7,000 m) of fabric.

PENCIL TIPS

Dalton Ghetti of Bridgeport, Connecticut, has been creating miniature graphite masterpieces from the tips of pencils for more than 25 years, including a sculpture of Elvis wearing shades, carved from a single pencil tip. He uses three tools—a razor blade, a sewing needle and a sculpting knife—but no magnifying glass. He digs into the graphite with the needle, then scratches and creates lines, turning the pencil slowly in his hand. One piece—a pencil with interlinking chains—took him two and a half years. He has made over 100 pencil-tip shapes in total, such as a saw, a screw, a key on a chain, a boot, a chair, a mini mailbox, and all 26 letters of the alphabet.

extraordinary art

BB-BALL GAGA

Sculptor and artist John O'Hearn of Gainesville, Florida, makes colorful mosaics from thousands of Airsoft BBs —the ¼-in (6-mm) plastic balls used in a BB gun. Among his designs are a portrait of Florida Gators quarterback Tim Tebow from 46,308 BBs, which measures 4 x 6 ft (1.2 x 1.8 m), and this larger-than-life mosaic of singer Lady Gaga that is 4 x 8 ft (1.2 x 2.4 m) and contains 61,509 BBs.

pothole scenes Urban artists Claudia Ficca and Davide Luciano from Montreal, Canada, travel North America transforming unsightly street potholes into works of art. They have been photographed in the guise of a woman washing her clothes in a pothole, a priest baptizing a baby in another, and a scuba diver taking a dip.

splendid sari A team of weavers in Chennai, India, spent 4,680 hours making a $100,000 sari, woven with precious metals and gems.

big monet At the 2010 Normandy Impressionist Festival, 1,250 fans of 19th-century French artist Claude Monet gathered in Rouen and held painted panels above their heads to create a giant, 6,460-sq-ft (600-sq-m) replica of his 1894 work *Rouen Cathedral at the End of the Day*. The result was captured by cameras perched 90 ft (27 m) above the city hall.

bone images Swiss-born artist and photographer Francois Robert, who is now based in the United States, produces works of art from real human bones. He spent hours arranging bones into striking shapes for his photographic collection *Stop the Violence*, which featured bone images of a gun, a tank, a bomb, a grenade, a Kalashnikov rifle, and a knife. He hit upon the idea after trading a wired-together human skeleton, found inside some school lockers he had bought, for a box of 206 human bones.

high horse Tony Dew from York, England, hand-carved a wooden rocking horse that stands 11 ft 10 in (3.6 m) high and 16 ft (4.9 m) long—more than twice the size of most real horses.

CART ART

Ptolemy Elrington trawls rivers and lakes near his studio in Brighton, England, for abandoned metal shopping carts and turns them into enchanting sculptures of animals, insects, and birds. By breaking up the carts and welding them into the desired shapes, he has created such designs as a heron, a frog (with bulging eyes from the cart's wheels), a dragonfly with a 6-ft (1.8-m) wingspan, and this kingfisher eating a fish.

last suppers For his *Last Suppers* series, British artist James Reynolds re-created the final meals requested by American Death Row prisoners. He filled a succession of orange prison-issue trays with their genuine last meals, which included a single black olive; an onion, a packet of chewing gum and two bottles of Coke; and six raw eggs.

dirt shirts Remembering how they always used to end up with manure on their clothes when they helped on the family farm as kids, Patti Froman Maine of Corry, Pennsylvania, and her brother Sonny Froman designed a range of T-shirts that are deliberately coated in the stuff. Their CowChipShirts don't smell and come in colors such as Udder Rose and Silage Brown.

gold painting Russian artist Elena Zolotaya created a 10-ft-wide (3-m) picture painted entirely with 14-carat gold.

DECORATIVE RECYCLING

Florida-based artists Alain Guerra and Neraldo de la Paz create stunning sculptures from discarded clothing. They drape old garments over a wire frame to form colorful designs including a rainbow, a snake, and a series of clothing trees that represent all four seasons of the year.

tall order For a wager, Norway's Ola Helland collected over one million giraffe pictures in 440 days. He was backpacking through South America when, as a keepsake to remember all the new friends he had met, he asked each to draw him a giraffe. When a friend bet him he couldn't collect a million, Ola set up a website and was soon deluged with giraffe pictures from 106 countries, including a giraffe made from a banana, and another made out of bread.

new books Each year, in the United States alone, about 30 million trees are used to make paper to print new books.

turning heads After going bald in his twenties, Philip Levine of London, England, began using his scalp as a canvas for art. Every week, body painter Kat Sinclair transformed Philip's designs into a different piece of head art. He turned his head into a disco ball covered with 1,000 crystals, had it painted with flowers, cartoon characters, and smiley faces, and even had acupuncture needles inserted into his scalp in the shape of a butterfly.

many hands At the 2010 Baltimore Book Festival in Maryland, 512 people contributed to a single piece of art. Local author K. Michael Crawford erected an easel with a blank canvas and invited passersby to add to the picture.

HELPING HAND

For his painting *The Hand with the Golden Ring*, Norwegian artist Morten Viskum said he used the hand of a human corpse as a paintbrush. He claims that he's been working with a severed hand as a brush for over a decade, and uses it to apply animal blood, acrylic paints, and sometimes glitter to his canvases.

Morten Viskum, *The Hand with the Golden Ring II* : 2010.

comedy gig American comedian Bob Marley performed a 40-hour gig at the Comedy Connection in Portland, Maine, lasting 18 hours before having to repeat any jokes.

golden vuvuzela A Russian businessman bought an Austrian-made gold and diamond-encrusted vuvuzela horn for over $20,000. The plastic South African horns, sounded by soccer spectators at the 2010 World Cup, usually cost around $8 each.

embroidered map Textile artist Lucy Sparrow of Brighton, East Sussex, England, has embroidered a 97-sq-ft (9-sq-m) tapestry of the London Underground map. It took her 42 days to make the giant map, which is made up of 7,875 ft (2,400 m) of thread and 142 buttons.

head banger Jim Bartek of Maple Heights, Ohio, listened to the album *Nostradamus* by heavy metal band Judas Priest once a day for 524 days in a row.

Paperback Titles On the bookshelves of his home in Wiltshire, England, Steve Hare has a collection of more than 15,000 Penguin paperbacks—including the first 2,000 titles published following their introduction in 1935. He has been collecting them for more than 45 years and has enough books to fill two trucks.

beach carving London, England, artist Everton Wright, aka Evewright, carved an outline of a 2,600-ft (800-m) artwork in the sand of a beach in Cumbria using a garden rototiller. A team of 20 horses and riders were then invited to walk along the outline to make the tracks deeper. The design took 18 months to plan, but lasted for only five hours until the tide came in and washed it all away.

long title When environmentalist Shripad Vaidya from Nagpur, India, released an anthology of eco-friendly poems in March 2010, the book's title consisted of no fewer than 355 words.

street strummers More than 850 ukulele players gathered in a London, England, street to play the Beach Boys' "Sloop John B" at the London Ukulele Festival in 2009.

cozy car Twenty grandmothers from Switzerland spent two months knitting nearly 70 lb (32 kg) of yarn into a warm covering for a Smart car. The woolen car cover depicts a lace-up training shoe but exposes the car's wheels, giving it the appearance of a giant roller skate.

junk sculptures James Corbett of Ningi, Queensland, Australia, makes amazing sculptures out of old car parts that he picks up from junkyards. He's turned discarded spark plugs, exhaust pipes, and radiators into such diverse artworks as a monkey, a yacht, a downhill skier, a kangaroo, and, appropriately, a heavy metal guitarist.

RUBBER BEASTS

Artist Ji Yong-Ho from Seoul, South Korea, makes animal sculptures from old tires. Using the flexibility of the rubber to imitate skin and muscles, he has created powerful lions, dogs, rhinos, and this 10-ft-long (3-m) shark, each work taking three months to make and selling for up to $75,000. To vary the skin texture, he uses different kinds of tread. For example, the neck and forehead of his rhinoceros are made from broad-treaded tractor tires layered beneath a rough outer skin of motorcycle tires.

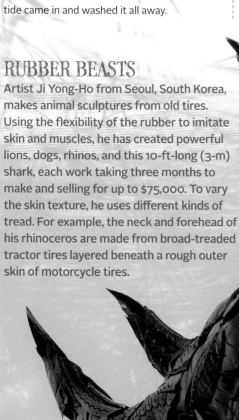

Curioser Creation

Los Angeles art group LA Pop Art wrote out every word from the first 11 chapters of Lewis Carroll's novel, Alice In Wonderland, to create an illustration from the story. From a distance it appears to be solid color, but almost every inch of the artwork is formed from Lewis Carroll's own words, written clearly in felt-tip pens. The text was written upside down so that the artists didn't smudge the ink.

painting with wheels Ian Cook of Birmingham, England, created an artwork of a racing car 33 x 16½ ft (10 x 5 m)—painted with the wheels of remote-control cars, go-karts, a racing car, a sports car, a motorbike, and a six-ton truck. He took a huge canvas, applied paint and then drove across it, creating the image with the different sizes and patterns of the tires. He said painting with the truck was particularly challenging because the back wheels were twice as wide as the front ones so it was difficult to see what he was doing.

guitar windmills Mimicking The Who guitarist Pete Townshend's windmill actions, Spencer Borbon of San Francisco whirled his arm around 79 times in 30 seconds at the 2009 San Francisco Treasure Island Music Festival.

tracker bob Bob "Tracker Bob" Hiemenz of Flora, Illinois, has a collection of more than 60,000 eight-track audio tapes. Since acquiring his first tapes in 1985, he has spent about $7,000 on his passion, which covers everyone from Abba to ZZ Top.

Sore Jaw Ken Parsons sang karaoke for more than two days straight at a church in Moose Jaw, Saskatchewan, Canada, in 2010. He finally put down the microphone after singing popular songs for an incredible 55 hours 11 minutes 30 seconds.

bard boost Performing William Shakespeare plays to cows can help boost milk production. After the Changeling Theatre Company entertained Friesian cows at a farm in Kent, England, with The Merry Wives of Windsor, milk yields increased by 4 percent.

finger portraits U.K.-based artist Kyle Lambert creates amazingly lifelike portraits of celebrities, including Jennifer Aniston and Beyoncé, using his fingers on an iPad.

sand sculpture A group of 30 artists took 75 days to create a 73-ft-tall (22-m) sand sculpture at the Zhoushan Sand Sculpture Festival in China. The sculpture depicted a Nigerian story of how a hummingbird managed to become king of all animals.

Inflated Animals

Chinese artist Yang Maoyuan creates animal sculptures with a difference—he takes the skins of dead animals and inflates them to monstrous sizes, often dyeing them in lurid colors.

Beijing-based Yang travels to Hebei in northern China to buy horse, goat, and sheep skins. He then stitches and processes the skins before blowing them up so that their bodies become bloated and round. He chooses animals from his Mongolian ancestry, making them larger than life to reflect his oldest dream symbols, and gives them a round shape that represents harmony in China. To make his sculptures even more grotesque, he gives some of the creatures two or three heads.

Yang's art has been a hit in galleries worldwide.

Yang's bright blue, three-headed, many-legged goat.

◀◀◀ **After**

Yang takes complete horse skins (right) **and turns them into works of art that symbolize his philosophy and the nomadic traditions of his ancestors.**

Before ▶▶▶

Tabletop Landscapes

New Jersey photographer and artist Matthew Albanese devises spectacular images of windswept tropical islands, tornadoes, and volcanoes by building models from everyday items.

The azure sea in his tabletop D.I.Y. Paradise is actually melted sugar and tin foil, and the island is made from salt. He carefully arranged cotton balls over the scene to create clouds, and even the palm trees are not as they seem—the leaves are formed from feathers.

Matthew has also made convincing icebergs from sugar and waterfalls from salt, and re-created the surface of Mars with paprika, cinnamon, nutmeg, and chili powder. His tornadoes are made from steel wool and he has created an impressive Aurora Borealis using a shower curtain, a corkboard, and strobe lighting. His photographs of these homemade natural phenomena sell for over $900 each.

® **ticket tower** British artist Robert Bradford created scale models of three U.K. landmarks—St. Paul's Cathedral, Edinburgh Castle, and Blackpool Tower—from a total of 115,000 used train tickets.

® **moon scent** Printers in Edinburgh, Scotland, have created a scratch 'n' sniff artwork that smells like the Moon. They developed it by talking to former NASA astronaut Charlie Duke, who was a member of the Apollo 16 mission in 1972, and who described the Moon's surface as smelling like spent gunpowder.

® **victory at last** Using an original wooden beam from the H.M.S. *Victory,* sculptor Ian Brennan from Hampshire, England, spent 17 years carving a 47-in-long (1.2-m) model of Admiral Horatio Nelson's 18th-century flagship. The model, accurate to the last detail, contains 200 ft (60 m) of rope, 104 miniature guns, and 37 sails.

® **cow maze** In a field near Berlin, Germany, workers cut corn and hemp into the shape of a giant cow. The maze depicted the bovine digestive system and was designed by the country's Federal Institute of Risk Assessment to promote healthy eating habits.

® **screw mosaic** Saimir Strati spent two weeks creating a mosaic of a U.S. banknote 8 ft (2.4 m) high and 16 ft 1 in (4.9 m) long from 300,000 industrial screws. The giant bill features a portrait of the ancient Greek poet Homer in the center.

® **natural sculptures** Peter Riedel, an artist and photographer from Toronto, Canada, spent five hours creating 42 temporary outdoor sculptures in the city's Humber River by balancing rocks and boulders on top of each other. He never uses glue in his works but arranges the rocks so that they don't fall.

still famous In the year following his death on June 25, 2009, Michael Jackson's estate earned one billion dollars.

same shot Except for the duration of World War II, Ria van Dijk had a photograph taken of herself at the same shooting gallery in Tilburg, the Netherlands, every year for 74 years. The first picture was taken in 1936 when she was 16.

poem boxing Japan hosts the National Poem Boxing Championships where contestants fight it out with words in three-minute rounds. The poets step into a boxing ring and read out verses on a wide range of subjects, hoping to secure a win. In the final round, the last two combatants still standing must improvise a poem incorporating a random word the judges tell them to use.

tiny book Hassan Abed Rabbo of Beirut, Lebanon, owns a handwritten, unabridged version of the Islamic holy book, the Quran, which is so tiny it can rest on the tip of his finger. The book, which dates back hundreds of years, contains 604 pages adorned in gold ink and measures just 0.95 x 0.75 in (2.4 x 1.9 cm).

young picasso A distinctive painting style of bold colors and disjointed Cubist forms led to ten-year-old Hamad Al Humaidhan from Bath, Somerset, England, being hailed as a young Picasso—even though he had never seen any of the Spanish master's work. The Kuwaiti-born youngster began painting at age seven, his first six pieces selling for $1,000 each. He closes his eyes, sees an image in his head, and then transfers it to the canvas.

ardent fan Over a period of nearly 20 years, Ann Petty of Wiltshire, England, has traveled more than 60,000 mi (100,000 km) to see Irish singer Daniel O'Donnell perform—including trips to the United States, New Zealand, and Australia.

log pile Logger Ron Fahey began removing a stack of logs from the grounds of Mount Allison University, Sackville, Canada, only to be stopped by an official who told him he was dismantling a work of art. The woodpile sculpture, called *Deadwood Sleep* by Paul Griffin, had been in the grounds for three years.

one-armed d.j. In Johannesburg, South Africa, in 2010, dance D.J. Nkosinathi Maphumulo, who lost his left hand in an accident at age 13, spun records for 60 hours straight with just a short comfort break every four hours.

clogged streets More than 2,500 people gathered in Pella, Iowa, on May 8, 2010, to dance together in wooden shoes.

phone-book furniture Daniel Tosches of Pasco, Florida, creates furniture and sculptures from pages of the phone book.

APPLE KILLER

Together with photographer Paul Fairchild, San Francisco artist Michael Tompert staged an exhibition of butchered and mangled Apple products. Tompert has shot, burned, hammered, and sawed his way through a range of merchandise and even ran over seven iPods with a diesel locomotive. His greatest challenge was an iPad, which survived a series of blows from a sledgehammer, before finally exploding after its insides were heated with a soldering torch. He says he's trying to make people think about their relationship with these highly popular items.

chocolate train In October 2010, London, England, food artist Carl Warner unveiled the *Chocolate Express*, a 6-ft (1.8-m) train sculpture made from chocolate, and running on chocolate tracks. It took ten days to build and also incorporated chocolate rolls, Wagon Wheels, Crunchie bars, and Dime bars.

lord of the sticks Patrick Acton of Gladbrook, Iowa, spent three years building a replica of the *Lord of the Rings* city Minas Tirith from 420,000 matchsticks.

photographic memories Munish Bansal of Kent, England, has taken pictures of his children every day for 13 years. He has filled more than 600 albums with over 8,500 digital images of his daughter Suman, 12, and her 10-year-old brother, Jay, since the day they were born.

part art Artist Franco Recchia from Florence, Italy, constructs models of cityscapes from the discarded parts of old computers. He uses circuit boards, casings, processing chips, and other computer components as his building blocks.

golden monopoly San Francisco jewelry designer Sidney Mobell has created a Monopoly set made with solid gold and jewels. The dice are encrusted with diamonds and these alone cost $10,000.

girl gucci At just 13 years old, Cecilia Cassini of Encino, California, is already an accomplished fashion designer. After receiving a sewing machine for her sixth birthday, she went on to design clothes for children and adults, and a number of celebrities have worn her designs.

toast portrait Laura Hadland from Leicester, England, created a portrait of her mother-in-law, Sandra Whitfield, from 9,852 slices of toast. Laura and 40 friends used nine toasters to brown the slices from 600 loaves of bread to varying degrees before arranging them to make a lifelike mosaic measuring 32 ft 8 in x 42 ft 3 in (10 x 13 m).

intrepid builder Using 250,000 pieces of LEGO®, Ed Diment took nine months to build a 22-ft-long (6.7-m) replica of the World-War-II aircraft carrier U.S.S. *Intrepid* in the conservatory of his home in Portsmouth, England. The finished model weighed more than 500 lb (227 kg).

porcelain seeds In 2010, London's Tate Modern gallery staged a work called *Sunflower Seeds* by Chinese artist Ai Weiwei. The piece consisted of more than 100 million individually handmade porcelain replicas of seeds.

party pooper With the help of local schoolchildren from Sichuan Province, China, sculptor Zhu Cheng made a replica of the famous *Venus de Milo* statue—from panda dung. The poop statue later sold for $45,000.

Plastic Fantastic

Sayaka Ganz creates amazing wildlife sculptures from items of discarded plastic found in garbage cans, thrift shops, or donated by friends—and her finished works sell for more than $12,000.

Sayaka, who was born in Japan but now lives in Fort Wayne, Indiana, has made models of penguins, an eagle, a horse, a cheetah, and a fish, varying in length from 18 in (45 cm) to 8 ft (2.4 m) and incorporating plastic sunglasses, cutlery, baskets, and cooking utensils. The biggest sculptures contain up to 500 pieces of junk and take nine months to make. She sorts all her plastic into 20 color groups in her basement and then ties the chosen items onto a wire frame to create each sculpture. Sayaka studies photographs showing her animal subjects from different angles so that she can perfect the lines of motion. She says, "I get great satisfaction from fitting these objects together to create a beautiful form that seems alive."

underground music Norwegian singer Unni Lovlid staged two sell-out 2010 concerts in a Victorian drain 20 ft (6 m) underground in Brighton, England. The sewer could accommodate 25 audience members wearing hard hats.

a klingon carol A Chicago, Illinois, theater staged a 2010 production of Charles Dickens' *A Christmas Carol*—entirely in Klingon. Written by Christopher O. Kidder and Sasha Walloch, the adaptation was performed in "tlhIngan Hol," the language of the Klingon race developed by linguist Marc Okrand for the 1984 movie *Star Trek III: The Search for Spock*.

spoon tree Students from Transworld University, Taiwan, made a 40-ft-tall (12-m) Christmas tree from 80,000 KFC plastic spoons.

pistol puzzle GarE Maxton, a machinist-artist from Michigan, created a 125-piece metal puzzle sculpture that can be assembled into a working, muzzle-loading pistol.

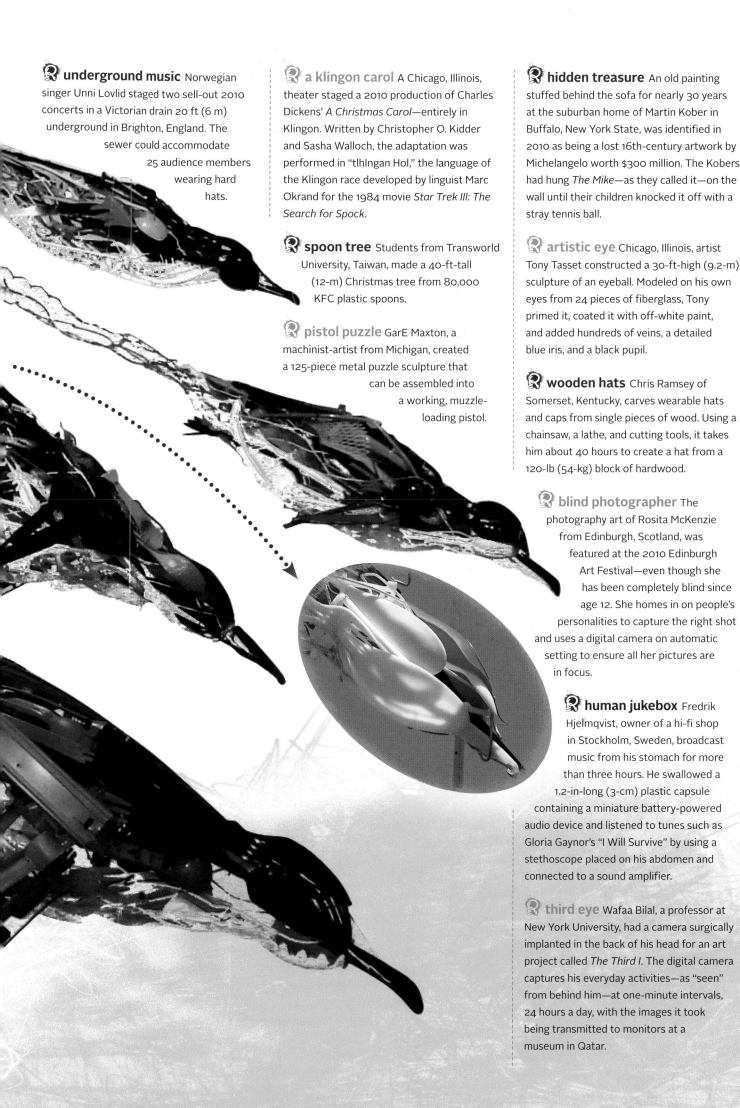

hidden treasure An old painting stuffed behind the sofa for nearly 30 years at the suburban home of Martin Kober in Buffalo, New York State, was identified in 2010 as being a lost 16th-century artwork by Michelangelo worth $300 million. The Kobers had hung *The Mike*—as they called it—on the wall until their children knocked it off with a stray tennis ball.

artistic eye Chicago, Illinois, artist Tony Tasset constructed a 30-ft-high (9.2-m) sculpture of an eyeball. Modeled on his own eyes from 24 pieces of fiberglass, Tony primed it, coated it with off-white paint, and added hundreds of veins, a detailed blue iris, and a black pupil.

wooden hats Chris Ramsey of Somerset, Kentucky, carves wearable hats and caps from single pieces of wood. Using a chainsaw, a lathe, and cutting tools, it takes him about 40 hours to create a hat from a 120-lb (54-kg) block of hardwood.

blind photographer The photography art of Rosita McKenzie from Edinburgh, Scotland, was featured at the 2010 Edinburgh Art Festival—even though she has been completely blind since age 12. She homes in on people's personalities to capture the right shot and uses a digital camera on automatic setting to ensure all her pictures are in focus.

human jukebox Fredrik Hjelmqvist, owner of a hi-fi shop in Stockholm, Sweden, broadcast music from his stomach for more than three hours. He swallowed a 1.2-in-long (3-cm) plastic capsule containing a miniature battery-powered audio device and listened to tunes such as Gloria Gaynor's "I Will Survive" by using a stethoscope placed on his abdomen and connected to a sound amplifier.

third eye Wafaa Bilal, a professor at New York University, had a camera surgically implanted in the back of his head for an art project called *The Third I*. The digital camera captures his everyday activities—as "seen" from behind him—at one-minute intervals, 24 hours a day, with the images it took being transmitted to monitors at a museum in Qatar.

extraordinary art

MAN-MADE MONSTERS

Using only manmade materials, Californian artist Doug Higley makes monsters for showmen to display at flea markets and fairs across the world. He has created fake mummified and petrified creatures, bogus mermaids, shrunken heads, chupacabras, freaky jungle pygmies, and atomic death worms. His work has been exhibited in 34 countries and one of his mermaids appeared at Buckingham Palace, London. He also once created 42 mermaids for a car-dealer promotion in the United States and Canada, whereby potential customers were invited to see the "strange creature" found in the trunk of a trade-in vehicle and take a test drive. The gimmick sold thousands of cars!

Water Dog Mermaid

Chupacabra

tentacle terror In 2008, artists Filthy Luker and Pedro Estrellas positioned huge inflatable green octopus tentacles through the windows of an unnamed building in France.

wooden chain Markley Noel of Hickory Corners, Michigan, carved a 480-ft-long (146-m) wooden chain from a single 25-ft-long (7.6-m) maple plank. The chain, which has 1,993 links, each 4 in (10 cm) long, took him seven years to make.

small portions Using acrylic paints and a magnifying glass, French artist Stephanie Kilgast creates miniature clay models of food in 1:12 scale. She painstakingly molds the clay with scalpels, blades, art knives, and toothpicks, and has made more than 600 cakes, pastries, fruit, and full meals, including a full English breakfast with baked beans, bacon, sausages, and fried eggs.

phone dress A London fashion company has introduced the M-Dress, a little black dress that also serves as a mobile phone. The dress, which has a tiny antenna in its hem, allows wearers to make and receive calls by putting their SIM card under the label. To take a call, they raise their hand to their ear; to end it they let it fall to their side.

ancient shoe Archeologists in Armenia have found a leather shoe more than 5,500 years old. The shoe, which was stuffed with grass, was discovered in a mountain cave where it had been kept in excellent condition thanks to a thick layer of sheep excrement, which acted as a protective seal.

corn maze Bob Connors cut images of Stewie and Brian, two of the characters from the animated TV comedy *Family Guy*, into a seven-acre cornfield maze at his farm in Danvers, Massachusetts.

fashion ferrari A full-size replica of a Ferrari Formula-1 car was made out of $60,000 worth of designer clothing. Eight people worked for five hours at a store in London's Carnaby Street to turn 1,999 items of clothing—including 1,682 red T-shirts, 88 pairs of jeans, 64 pairs of shoes, and 31 belts—into a 14-ft-long (4.3-m) model car. The wheels were made from water bottles, the wing mirrors from sunglasses, and the tires from black jeans.

Deep Drawings

Chilean artist Fredo creates mind-boggling 3-D pencil drawings that appear to rise out of the page. Despite its 3-D appearance, all his work is pencil on flat paper. At only 17 years old, Fredo is already exhibiting his work in Chile.

strand of beads In October 2009, the city of Providence, Rhode Island, created a strand of red-and-white beads that measured 1,349 ft (411 m) long!

late returns In 2009, a former student at Camelback High School, Phoenix, Arizona, returned two library books that had been checked out half a century earlier, and enclosed a $1,000 money order for the fines. The books had been taken out in 1959, but the borrower's family moved to another state and the books were mistakenly packed away.

toothpick city Scott Weaver of Rohnert Park, California, spent thousands of hours during a 34-year period building a toothpick model of every major landmark in San Francisco, using a total of over 100,000 toothpicks. The construction, titled "Rolling Through the Bay," stands 9 ft (2.7 m) tall, 7 ft (2.1 m) wide and 2 ft (60 cm) deep. It has survived four house relocations, an earthquake, and Trooper—one of Weaver's four Great Danes—who once obliterated Fisherman's Wharf and about 100 hours' work with a careless wag of his tail.

human hoover Artist Paul Hazelton of Kent, England, has made a model of a complete bedroom—including a TV, armchairs, and a wardrobe—out of dust! Known as the "Human Hoover," he collects dust from furniture, pictures, and window sills, and then transforms the bunches of tiny particles into 3-D sculptures by wetting, shaping, and drying them. Some of his dust models—which also include a briefcase, a moth, and a humanoid—are 20 in (50 cm) high.

hot lips Makeup artist Rick DiCecca applied lipstick to over 300 women in one hour at Macy's Department Store, Chicago, Illinois.

lego ship For nearly a week, 3,500 children used 513,000 LEGO® bricks to build a 25-ft-long (7.6-m) model of a container ship in Wilhelmshaven, Germany.

DISK PORTRAITS

British artist Nick Gentry uses old 3.5-in computer floppy disks as a canvas for his imaginative portraits. The features of each face are mapped into a grid, with each section the size of one disk. The disks are then arranged to create a collage before the outline of the head is partly drawn and painted over it. He sometimes also incorporates obsolete cassettes and V.C.R. tapes into his facial images.

monster mona A giant version of the *Mona Lisa* went on display in a shopping mall in Wrexham, Wales, in 2009—50 times bigger than Leonardo da Vinci's 16th-century original. It covered 2,600 sq ft (240 sq m) and was big enough to fit 22 buses inside. A total of 245 people worked on the project under artist Katy Webster, and it took 987 hours to create, using 23 gal (86 l) of paint.

wicker men In Cluj, Romania, a team of 16 craftsmen created a huge wicker basket that was large enough to hold one million loaves of homemade bread. It took nine days to make and measured 59 x 33 ft (18 x 10 m), and was 31 ft (9.5 m) tall.

celebrity pumpkins Gardener David Finkle carves impressive portraits of famous people—including Barack Obama, Michael Jackson, and Simon Cowell—out of pumpkins that grow on his small farm at Chelmsford in Essex, England.

concert for dogs Australia's Sydney Opera House staged a concert for dogs in 2010. More than a thousand dogs turned up for the 20-minute Music For Dogs event, which was organized by U.S. musician Laurie Anderson and her rock-star husband Lou Reed. It featured a concerto of high-pitch whistles, whale calls, synthesizers, and strings—some inaudible to human ears.

couscous city French-Algerian artist Kader Attia built a scale model of the ancient city of Ghardaia, Algeria, entirely out of cooked couscous.

dental display To entertain and relax his patients, dentist Ian Davis from London, England, has created a series of sculptures featuring miniature men scrubbing, cleaning, and repairing teeth. The men can be seen digging out fillings with tiny pickaxes and polishing and scaling teeth with the help of scaffolding—and all the teeth he uses are taken from the casts of real patients' mouths.

dollar mosaics A Latvian artist creates mosaics made entirely out of U.S. dollar bills. Irina Truhanova sketches an outline of her subject before filling it in with snippets of the bills. Her creations include the Statue of Liberty, a Bentley car, and Russian President Vladimir Putin.

urban dancers As part of its 2009 "Bodies in Urban Spaces" project, Dance Umbrella, choreographed by Willi Dorner, placed its performers in unlikely locations around the center of London, England. Passersby stumbled across dancers squeezed between pillars, wrapped around lampposts, folded into a bicycle rack, and clinging to a wall like Spider-Man.

typewriter art Cerebral-palsy sufferer Paul Smith of Roseburg, Oregon, who died in 2007, became a world-famous artist by creating masterpieces using manual typewriters. He achieved his amazing images by pressing the symbols at the tops of the number keys, and as his mastery of the typewriter grew, he developed techniques to create shadings, colors, and textures that made his work resemble pencil or charcoal drawings. Over the years, he created hundreds of artworks—each one taking him up to three months—including landscapes, animals, and portraits.

underwater gallery Diving enthusiasts in Lithuania have opened the country's first underwater picture gallery. Twenty large-format photographs by local artists were put on display beneath the surface of Lake Plateliai, and the organizers hope to expand the project to include sculptures, stained glass, and watercolor paintings. The idea originated after a couple from a diving club put their wedding picture underwater so that they could enjoy it every time they dived.

roadkill hats Fashion designer James Faulkner of Edinburgh, Scotland, has created a range of hats from roadkill. Inspired by the idea of using a dead magpie he found by the roadside to complement a friend's black-and-white dress, he has developed a range of 36 animal hats, using the wings, feathers, and fur of squashed pigeons, rabbits, foxes, pheasants, and crows.

27-hour concert Gonzales, a Canadian musician, played a 27-hour concert in Paris, France, in 2009. His 300-song set ranged from Britney Spears to Beethoven.

ant invasion Dutch artist Henk Hofstra painted some 500 giant red ants over the town of Drachten for his work "Invasion of the Ants." The ants—each 10 x 6½ ft (3 x 2 m) were created over three nights in May 2010 and were placed so that they appeared to be invading the De Lawei Theater, which was celebrating its 50th anniversary.

THE CANDY MAN

Mexican artist Cristiam Ramos makes amazing candy portraits of celebrities. Instead of paint, he uses Gummi Bears, licorice, M&M's®, and after-dinner mints as his artistic materials. His works include likenesses of Elvis and Michael Jackson from hundreds of M&M's®, and a portrait of Lady Gaga from gumdrops, M&M's®, and yellow licorice.

Mini Me

Indonesian photographer Ari Mahardika has "cloned" himself dozens of times for a series of intricate montages. Using a self-timer to take photos of himself in different poses against a white background, he then shrinks the portraits into mini-me characters, positioning them so that it looks as though he is interacting with himself.

lost movie A lost Charlie Chaplin film valued at $60,000 was bought on eBay for $5.68 by a British collector in 2009. Morace Park of Essex, England, purchased the battered olive green film canister listed as "an old film" and was amazed to discover that the movie in question was *Zepped*, a 1916 Chaplin propaganda film poking fun at the zeppelin, the German instrument of terror during World War I. As recently as 2006, a movie expert stated that the seven-minute movie had almost certainly been lost forever.

junior drummer At just three years of age, Howard Wong's rock drumming has attracted nearly ten million hits on YouTube even though he can barely see over the top of his drum kit. Howard from Penang, Malaysia, first started playing at the age of 18 months and now performs regularly with his father's band.

bean mosaic A candy shop in Brighton, England, displayed a colorful mosaic of Queen Elizabeth II made from 10,000 jelly beans.

first exhibition When Leo Haines was born with cerebral palsy and a terminal condition affecting his lungs and heart, he was given only six months to live. However, in 2010 the five-year-old from Somerset, England, stunned doctors by opening his first art exhibition. He began painting alongside his grandmother and has since completed more than 40 works, which are said to be reminiscent of famous U.S. abstract artist Jackson Pollock.

Gum Dog

Gareth Williams of the U.K. created this sculpture of a dog, which was exhibited at London's Royal College of Art in 2009, with hair clippings from his own head stuck together with pieces of used chewing gum.

same glass For more than 35 years on an almost daily basis, Peter Dreher of Wittnau, Germany, has painted a portrait of the same drinking glass in the same position in his studio. He has so far completed more than 4,000 paintings of the glass.

lego repairs German artist Jan Vormann travels the world fixing crumbling walls and monuments with LEGO®. Among areas he has brightened up with the toy bricks are the old quarter of Tel Aviv in Israel and New York's Bryant Park.

midnight knitter Under the cover of darkness in early 2010, an unknown person dubbed the "Midnight Knitter" draped tree branches and lampposts in West Cape May, New Jersey, with small, brightly colored woolen sweaters.

cool music Norwegian composer Terje Isungset has recorded several albums with instruments made entirely of ice, including percussion, horns, and trumpets.

movie veteran Aachi Manorama, a veteran of India's Tamil film industry, has appeared in more than 1,500 movies and 1,000 stage performances.

early watch In 2009, art experts discovered a 450-year-old painting that featured an image of a watch. The portrait, painted by Italian Renaissance artist Maso da San Friano around 1560, shows Cosimo I de' Medici, Duke of Florence, holding a golden timepiece. Watches first appeared shortly after 1500, making this one of the oldest paintings to depict a true watch.

tower cozy Robyn Love of New York City crocheted a yarn cozy for a wooden water tower on Broadway. Over a period of three weeks, she and six assistants used 60 balls of yellow and black yarn to transform the tower into a huge yellow pencil, complete with point.

sitting in silence Over a period of nearly three months in 2010, Serbian performance artist Marina Abramović spent 700 hours simply sitting and staring across a table at members of the public at New York's Museum of Modern Art. She sat on a chair for seven hours a day, six days a week, for her installation *The Artist Is Present*. Around 1,400 people—including singer Björk and model Isabella Rossellini—sat opposite her and returned her silent gaze. Some managed an entire day; others lasted just a few minutes.

expensive doll A French doll designed by Paris artist Albert Marque in 1915 was sold at auction in Atlanta, Georgia, for $263,000 in 2009. Only 100 examples of the doll were ever made and each was individually costumed, in styles ranging from 18th-century French court to traditional Russian folklore.

hay castle In January 2010, visitors flocked to Rob Marshall's sheep farm in West Victoria, Australia, to see a castle measuring 100 x 20 ft (30 x 6 m) that he had built out of hundreds of bales of hay. The castle remained in situ for six weeks until Rob dismantled it and used the bales to feed his sheep.

tree sculpture Inspired by a silver birch tree, Swedish furniture chain IKEA created a huge tree sculpture made from white kitchen appliances—including a washing machine, a dishwasher, and a microwave oven—that was erected outside London's Barbican Centre in 2010.

holiday snaps A series of 19th-century watercolor paintings of European beauty spots by an unknown female British holidaymaker was sold in London for more than $5,000 in 2010. The paintings of such picturesque locations as Bavaria, the Swiss Alps, and the Belgian city of Bruges were made in journals as holiday snaps by the woman following vacations she took with her husband in 1850 and 1853.

Ripley's Ask

Why did you start using your own blood for your paintings? I guess the easiest answer would be to prove to myself that I could. I have used every medium I could think of during the course of my artistic career, from oil paint, charcoal, graphite, automotive paints, inks, even coffee, so I think it was just to see if I could.

After my first one, I was so proud of my work and fascinated by the finish, even though my first one was somewhat clumsy in its execution, so I set off on my journey to perfect my blood work. And with each painting, I learned how to predict how it would handle on various surfaces, how it changes and how my blood itself varies depending on things like diet, hydration, and so on.

How much blood do you use in a typical painting? This really depends on the image. As a guide, a 20 x 20 in (500 x 500 mm) painting will use between $1^1/_2$ fl oz (40 ml) and $6^3/_4$ fl oz (200 ml). It also depends on the tools I use—for example, airbrushed textures use a lot less than a paintbrush.

How much blood do you extract on a regular basis? Earlier on I was extracting up to twice per week. However, years of doing so has caused scar tissue in my vein walls so it is becoming increasingly painful to remove, so when we do, we take a lot, up to 1 pint (440 ml) at a time and then I store it in the refrigerator.

Is blood easy to use? How does it compare to regular ink? Not even close, it is by far the most difficult substance to use. It is not actually red—the cells within the plasma are—so essentially I'm painting with my body's tissue. These cells clog airbrushes, and don't give uniform coverage from a brush—once dry even the smallest amount of moisture will liquefy it again, so it's very easy to "burn" through what you have already painted. It has taken me a long time to master what I have, and I have almost completely given up all other mediums now because my blood painting has been deeply rewarding and proven very popular worldwide.

Blood Painter

Rev Mayers never runs out of the unique ink he uses for his paintings, because it's one hundred percent his own blood on the canvas. The extreme artist from Sydney, Australia, has the blood extracted from his arm using a syringe, just as a doctor would. He then applies the precious fluid with an airbrush or a standard paintbrush. More detail and depth becomes visible as the art ages. Rev estimates that he has so far used more than 12 pints of his own blood in his paintings, more than most adults have in their entire body.

ACKNOWLEDGMENTS

COVER (t/l) LA Pop Art www.lapopart.com, (b/l) Insaland.com; 4 LA Pop Art www.lapopart.com; 6–7 Pictures courtesy of Craig Tracy; 8 (t) Victor Liu/Solent News/Rex Features, (b) Images courtesy of Shauna Richardson; 9 Caters News; 10 (t) Solent News/Rex Features, (b/l, b) Geoffrey Robinson/Rex Features; 11 (t/r) Kris Kuksi, (b/r) Geoffrey Robinson/Rex Features; 12–13 Kris Kuksi; 14 Bernard Pras; 15 (t) Xia Xiao Wan, (b) Insaland.com; 16–17 Solent News/Rex features; 18 (b) Drew Gardner/eyevine; 19 (b, t/l, c/l) Images courtesy of Morten Viskum and VEGAS gallery, London, (t/r) Guerra de la Paz; 20 Ji Yong-Ho/Solent/Rex Features; 21 LA Pop Art www.lapopart.com; 22–23 Yang Maoyuan; 24 (l) Matthew Albanese, (t/l, t/r) matthewalbanese.com/Solent News/Rex Features; 24–25 (b) Michael Tompert/Paul Fairchild/Rex Features; 26–27 Solent News/Rex Features; 28 www.grindshow.com; 29 (t) Fredo, (b) Nick Gentry/Barcroft Media Ltd; 31 Ari Mahardhika/Solent News/Rex Features; 32 (t) Getty Images; 33 (sp) Dr Rev Bloodpainter, (t) © Mafaldita/istockphoto.com; BACK COVER www.grindshow.com

Key: t = top, b = bottom, c = center, l = left, r = right, sp = single page, dp = double page

All other photos are from Ripley Entertainment Inc.
Every attempt has been made to acknowledge correctly and contact copyright holders and we apologize in advance
for any unintentional errors or omissions, which will be corrected in future editions.